collective
Contemporary Styles Series

CD INCLUDED

Contemporary Rock Styles For the Drums

by Sandy Gennaro

T0078759

This book is dedicated to the loving memory of Sadie Gennaro.
Her unconditional love, support and encouragement have fueled the pursuit of my musical dreams.
Thanks Ma, I love and miss you.

thecollective is a world-class learning center for drumset players, percussionists, bassists, keyboardists and guitarists of all levels. We offer plans of study ranging from individual lessons and clinics to full-time programs of ten weeks to two-years in length. If you're serious about becoming the best musician you can be, we're serious about helping you accomplish that goal.

**541 Avenue of the Americas,
New York, NY 10011
T: 212-741-0091**

www.thecoll.com

Executive Producer – *Lauren Keiser*
Executive Co-producer – *John Costellano*
Author Liason – *Tony Maggiolino*
Creative Director – *Alex Teploff*
Managing Editor – *Nicholas Hopkins*
Production Editor – *Seth Goldberg*
Cover Design – *Andrew J. Dowty*
Book Design – *Andrew J. Dowty*
Production Designer – *Andy Ray Wong*
Photo of New York City – *Maureen Plainfield*
Other Photography – *Andy Dowty and Kyung Chul-Choi*
Production Coordinator and Audio Engineer – *Tony Conniff*

CARL FISCHER®

65 Bleecker Street, New York, NY 10012

ISBN 0-8258-6267-1

TABLE OF CONTENTS

Foreword 3

Introduction 3

Introduction to the Musical Style of Rock 'n' Roll 3

General Performance Tips 4

How to Use This Book..5

Drumkey Notation..5

About Sandy Gennaro..6

Sub-Style No. 1: Straight Eighth-Note Feel with Stop Time 7

Sub-Style No. 2: Medium Rock Stomp 11

Sub-Style No. 3: Rock Ballad 13

Sub-Style No. 4: Funk Rock 16

Sub-Style No. 5: Heavy Rock (Double Bass Drums)...20

Sub-Style No. 6: Traditional Shuffle 24

Sub-Style No. 7: Hard Rock Shuffle 27

Sub-Style No. 8: $\frac{12}{8}$ Slow Blues 30

Sub-Style No. 9: 2-Beat 33

Sub-Style No. 10: Train Beat (Country Shuffle) 36

Sub-Style No. 11: "Bo Diddley" Beat..39

Sub-Style No. 12: New Orleans Second Line 42

Sub-Style No. 13: Up-tempo Rock-Swing with Stop Time (Rockabilly) 45

Sub-Style No. 14: Reggae (Shuffle Feel)..48

Sub-Style No. 15: Rockin' Odd Meters 51

Selected Bibliography..54

Selected Discography 54

Glossary of Common Terms...55

Performers on the CD:

Sandy Gennaro – Drums
Gary Kelly – Bass
Kenny Brescia – Guitar

FOREWORD

The Collective was established in 1977 by a small group of professional New York musicians, who wanted to pool their energies and create a place where young drummers, and later bass, guitar, and keyboard students, could study and prepare themselves for a career in music. Since opening its doors, The Collective has graduated thousands of students, who have gone on to establish themselves in the world of professional music. I don't think that it is immodest to say that our alumni are helping to shape the direction that popular music is taking around the world.

Over the years the curriculum at The Collective has evolved to include a wide range of courses focusing on everything from technique and reading, to the study of all the important contemporary and ethnic styles. This book, along with our other Rhythm Section based books, covers the material offered in the Collective's Certificate Program.

The styles offered here represent the key styles in the contemporary idiom. Since all styles have tended to grow out of each other, and mutually influence each other, the student will find common threads that link them all together and make it easier to absorb and make them part of a young musician's personal style signature.

Each book contains a brief biography of the author, who is the faculty member who teaches this style at The Collective. You will also find a brief introduction to the general style and examples of the various substyles to be studied. Woven throughout the material are performance tips that come out of the teacher's years of experience. The most important element, however, are the pre-recorded rhythm-section CDs, on which our teachers perform with other musicians who also specialize in playing the style. Listening to and practicing with these CDs are the most important things for you to do to develop skills playing in the style. Music notation and the written word can, at best, only help you derive an intellectual understanding of the music. It is in listening to the actual music that you will come to understand it. In this regard, we strongly encourage you to make an effort to listen to the music listed in the recommended discography at the end of each section. The blank staves are meant for you to notate your own personal variations for each style. First, you must learn the pure style; then, you can adapt it to your own musical needs.

I would like to express my appreciation to all the teachers who have, over the years, contributed to the growth of the Collective and to this program in particular. I would also like to thank the hard working and talented folks at Carl Fischer for supporting our effort to get it right, and doing such a fine job with this book. Finally, I would like to thank Tony Maggiolino of our staff for all his hard work in coordinating all the material, and struggling to meet ever looming deadlines.

—John Castellano.
Director, The Collective

Introduction to the Musical Style of Rock 'n' Roll

Rock 'n' Roll, or simply Rock for our purposes, is one of the simplest and most basic forms of music yet at the same time being very complex, given its deep, diverse history of musical and rhythmic influences. The pioneers of Rock drew inspiration from Jazz, Big Band Swing, Gospel, Country, Folk, Reggae, New Orleans, Blues, Funk, African and Rockabilly. The style has evolved into a "melting pot" with two or more combining to form a "new" style and therefore influencing a new generation of musicians and songwriters. The music of Elvis Presley, for example, fused elements of Country, Gospel and Big Band Swing. His music then influenced the likes of the Beatles and the Rolling Stones. These groups formed the core of what was known as the "British Invasion," which changed the face of American music and culture forever.

4

In the 1930s and 40s Big Band Swing Orchestras, such as Tommy Dorsey and Benny Goodman, were prominent. Several of these bands featured vocalists, such as Frank Sinatra, Tony Bennett and Bing Crosby, who eventually became solo artists in there own right. These singers often filled theaters with legions of screaming teenage fans twenty years before what became known as "Beatlemania." This is important to recognize because the swing pulse is the common denominator of all American music. Early 50s Rock had a heavy swing pulse with a "2 & 4" backbeat. Eventually, the feel started to even out due largely to Boogie Woogie piano players who would play a feel somewhere between a shuffle and eighth notes. By 1956 or '57 drummers were playing a straight eighth-note feel with a backbeat. By the mid 50s you had artists who fronted their own small bands of sidemen. These artists include Bo Diddley, Bill Haley, Elvis, Buddy Holly, Jerry Lee Lewis, Little Richard, Fats Domino and Chuck Berry, all of whom carried on in the Swing, Blues and Country tradition. In the early 60s The Beatles rose to fame. They were influenced largely by the solo artists of the 50s and Ska, which was an up-tempo reggae style that existed in England in the 50s. What made The Beatles unique at the time was that they were the first group to write, perform and sing their own songs.

Following The Beatles in the late 60s and into the 70s were the Rolling Stones (blues, swing, country), Cream (blues, swing) Led Zeppelin (blues, folk), The Who (sheer mayhem) and Jimi Hendrix (swing, blues). At the same time you had groups evolving out of the James Brown, Funk, Blues and R&B lineage such as Sly Stone, Tower of Power and, later, Prince. You also had artists being born out of the Folk/Country/Blues tradition such as Bob Dylan, The Byrds, the Grateful Dead and Janis Joplin. Each generation produced a new "hybrid" based on the music of the prior generations.

General Performance Tips

Rock drumming relies heavily on consistency of tempo and independence. It's all about feel and simplicity. Practicing technique for technique's sake is not the answer. Having a large "palette" of musical ideas (beats, fills etc.) from which to draw and to utilize these ideas appropriately in song situations is the key. It's not how much you play; it's what you play where. It's what you don't play. Space, groove, feeling and heart—this is Rock 'n' Roll.

Being "friends" with time-keeping devices such as metronomes, drum machines and sequencers is of paramount importance. They are used almost all the time in the studio, and more and more artists are using them live to sequence background vocals, percussion, horn parts etc.

I think the utilization of the hi-hat foot as a timekeeper is vital to consistency. More than a "2 & 4" is necessary to achieve this; namely, quarter notes or upbeats in medium to bright tempos and in medium to slow tempos, or where more complicated bass drum patterns are utilized are places where I play my left foot in eighth notes. We keep the pulse with our left heel when we are riding on the hi-hat with our right hand. All other times, we keep the pulse on the hi-hat as we normally do, by playing with our left foot.

As mentioned in the introduction, the swing pulse is the root of all Rock, so the development of a variety of shuffles is essential.

- The use of dynamics within the song is of the utmost importance.
- Practice in a variety of dynamic levels and tempos.
- Practice rhythms in increments of 4 bars (4, 8, 12, 16 etc.), because most rock songs are written this way. **Never play fills or crashes over a vocal,** except when directed to do so.
- Develop a consistent rim shot for the backbeat and really soft ghost notes for the in-between strokes.

Pulse is what we base our feel on. **Time** is what keeps that pulse steady. Without the pulse, we are merely playing a collection of notes in time with no feel. Pulse can be straight, it can swing or it can be somewhere in between.

Maintain a positive attitude, the ability to take direction and the willingness to serve the artist/producer that you are working for. This is sometimes more important than the actual playing—the attitude with which you play it.

A successful Rock drummer is a team player that plays what the song needs, nothing more, and plays it confidently, with emotion, heart, consistency and a positive attitude.

You rock!

How to Use This Book

- The demo of each sub-style includes the drums playing portions of each section of the chart. The play-along section includes the entire chart of the sub-style performed by the bassist and guitar player and includes a click track for you to play along with.
- Make note of the various "roadmaps" provided for each chart and demo.
- Listen to the demo of the sub-style while reading the chart to familiarize yourself with the groove and the feel of each track.
- Read along with the charts of each sub-style while listening to the corresponding track on the CD.
- Always play the charts and optional beats first without the CD or a metronome to get the "mechanics" and the feel of the material being played. Be sure each limb is doing the correct part cleanly and comfortably before you proceed.
- If the indicated tempo of any chart prohibits you from playing it cleanly and effectively, set your metronome to a slower tempo and play the chart without the CD. Gradually increase your metronome tempo until you reach the tempo of the chart. It will also benefit you to perform the chart with your metronome set at a faster tempo than indicated on the chart. Then play it at a slower tempo than the one indicated.
- What? You don't have a metronome? Stop reading this **immediately** and get your butt down to the nearest music store and get one—**now!** Bring your headphones to make sure they fit the headphone input on the metronome and to make sure the metronome is loud enough to hear the clicks over the sound of your acoustic drums.
- Play the optional beats without the metronome first, then with it at various tempos.
- Experiment with substituting the optional beats for the beats written in the chart.
- Start with the metronome at a very slow tempo, say 40 beats per minute (bpm), then increase the tempo by 10 bpm and play the material again.
- Every time you rehearse, select a different starting point for your metronome practice. Today, start at 40 bpm then go to 50, 60, 70 etc. tomorrow start at 45 bpm then go to 55, 65, 75 etc. After awhile, you will be comfortable playing in virtually every tempo of the metronome. **Why?** Because there are songs that fit just about every tempo of the metronome.
- When you practice, play the material in specific numbers of measures say, 4, 8, 12, 16, and 24. Why? Because sections of songs are commonly written in this manner.
- Repetition. Repetition, and repetition is the key in making anything you rehearse a part of your everyday playing vocabulary.
- Smile, relax and maintain a positive attitude knowing that you will be a better drummer tomorrow than you are today.

Drumkey Notation

About Sandy Gennaro

Born and raised in New York City, I have been a member of the Drummers Collective faculty since 1987. My successful DCI/ Warner Bros Instructional video/DVD titled *Drum Basics* has been certified platinum.

I have had the privilege of "tutoring" Lionel Hampton after his stroke. I have "tutored" Peter Criss of KISS prior to KISS tours and recording sessions.

I have recorded or toured with Cyndi Lauper, Joan Jett & the Blackhearts, The Pat Travers Band, Bo Diddley, Johnny Winter, Jon Paris, Michel Bolton, The Monkees, The Bee Gees, Little Steven van Zandt, Benny Mardones, The Mamas & Papas, Steppenwolf, Lou Christie, Martha & The Vandellas, Leslie Gore, Craaft and Seiko Higuchi among others.

Please visit www.sandygennaro.com for more information, many great photos and a way to contact me. I welcome any and all comments, suggestions and questions. Thank you, and I hope you enjoy this book/CD.

I would like to thank:
DW Drums and Pedals
Paiste Cymbals
Hot Sticks
Remo
Rhythm Tech Percussion
SKB Cases
John Castellano and the staff of the Drummers Collective
Rob Wallis and Paul Seigal
Seth Goldberg and the staff of Carl Fischer Music

SUB-STYLE NO. 1:
Straight Eighth-Note Feel with Stop Time

Brief History

By the middle 1940s the swing pulse included a strong backbeat. Boogie Woogie piano players of the late 1940s and early 1950s interpreted the swing pulse as being somewhere in between the shuffle and the eighth note. This "new" feel influenced the drummer of the day who eventually took it all the way over to the eighth-note side. Then in the 60s some of the more accomplished players took the kick drum to sixteenth-note world and things got very interesting. The earliest example of the "in-between" feel featuring Stop Time, the Rock form with intros and outros and a "walking" bass line, is a tune by Benny Goodman called *Boy Meets Goy*. It was recorded in 1940. Listen to this track—it, in my opinion, is where it all began.

Another fine example of the straight eighth Boogie Shuffle with Stop-Time, a 12-bar form is a song I perform nightly with The Monkees called *No Time*. There are literally dozens of tunes that utilize this form with its intro and outro, which is why it's important for any Rock drummer to "own" this style. It is one of the building blocks of Rock.

Performance Tips

- Utilize strong backbeat.
- Master the art of the rim shot.
- Explore the many different sound possibilities on the snare drum utilizing different points of attack on the snare head (rim shot and non rim shot) and different points on the shaft of the stick to execute a rim shot.
- Use optional endings.
- Play with dynamics between sections.
- Keep time with left foot: simple beats in bright tempos use quarter notes. In more complicated grooves using sixteenth notes and sixteenth-note triplets on the kick drum played at slower tempos, use eighth notes on the left foot, as explained in detail in the **General Performance Tips** section on page 4.
- When playing quarter bell ride or the upbeat bell ride, produce a nice, strong bell sound by playing the bell using the shoulder of the stick.
- Where indicated, play ghost notes very softly and the accents very loudly.
- When playing an open/closed hi-hat, open the hi-hat where indicated by the small circle (o) and tightly close it on the following eighth note. This has to be executed cleanly and crisply in order to be effective.
- Rehearse this groove with a metronome at a variety of tempos.

Class Notes:

8

Straight Eighth-Note Feel with Stop Time

Demo Roadmap
Intro, A, B, C

Chart Roadmap
Intro-A-B (3X), C

Class Notes: _____

_____

_____

Straight Eighth-Note Feel Variations

Selected Recorded Examples

Great Balls of Fire – Jerry Lee Louis
Johnny B. Goode – Chuck Berry, Johnny Winter (Live)
Let the Good Times Roll – Jimi Hendrix
Lucille – Little Richard
No Time – The Monkees
Oh Carol – The Rolling Stones
Rock and Roll – Led Zeppelin
This House is Rockin' – Stevie Ray Vaughn

Class Notes:

Class Notes:

Class Notes:

Class Notes:

SUB-STYLE NO. 2:
Medium Rock Stomp

Brief History

A strong snare played on the quarter-note downbeat—1, 2, 3, 4—identifies this groove. It is most commonly heard today in hard rock. When played in faster tempos we hear it in heavy metal and speed metal. Starting back in the late 1950s, this very infectious groove was used very often by Rhythm & Blues songwriters, singers and drummers alike. In all likelihood, it dates back to the 1920s on some back porch of a little shack in Tupelo, Mississippi. A small group was singing the praises to the Lord, clapping their hands on the quarter note until they couldn't clap anymore. This feel is the downbeat counterpart of the 2-beat, upbeat stomp—the core of the Gospel feel.

Performance Tips

- Develop the very deep pocket by playing quarters with kick and snare (no rim shot) and eighths with the right hand on the hi-hat played with the tip of the stick, not the shoulder.
- When there is a pre-determined bass guitar part for a song, explore the three possibilities for a kick drum part: 1. Play the same rhythm as the bass guitar. 2. Create a sparse "bed" rhythm over which he can lay his bass rhythm. 3. Play the kick drum "in between" or "counter" the bass guitar rhythm.
- Pay attention to the clean execution of the open/closed hi-hat.
- Practice these grooves with a metronome at various tempos.

Medium Rock Stomp
CD Track #3 Demo / Track #4 Play-along

Demo Roadmap
Intro, A, B, C

Chart Roadmap
Intro-A-B (4X), C

Medium Rock Stomp Variations

Selected Recorded Examples

Crossroads (*Live*) – *Wheels of Fire* album - Cream
Dance to the Music – Sly and the Family Stone
Deuce – KISS
Don't Bring Me Down – The Animals
Go My Way – Lenny Kravitz
(I Can't Get No) Satisfaction – The Rolling Stones
I Can't Turn You Loose – The Blues Brothers
Pretty Woman – Roy Orbison, Van Halen
Reflections – The Supremes

SUB-STYLE NO. 3:
Rock Ballad

Brief History

The earliest ballads that were popular in the 50s existed in the blues or $\frac{12}{8}$ form in the same way the shuffle preceded the eighth-note form of Rock. Even though the song may have been a "pop" tune it was still written in a triplet, $\frac{12}{8}$ or blues form. When drummers started using straight eighths with a backbeat in the middle to late 50s, this paved the way for the eighth-note rock ballad.

The focus when playing this feel is the vocal. The general rule is "if it gets in the way of the vocal line, don't play it." This is the way producer Barry Mraz put it to me prior to the recording of Benny Mardones' Top 10 single *Into the Night*. He said to play simply, behind the beat and with an R&B feel. It's one of the few songs that became a Top Ten single on two separate occasions, ten years apart. It has since become a classic, being played in elevators, hotel lobbies, and supermarkets—anywhere recorded music is played. The drum track was recorded in about three takes, without a click track.

Another dynamic performance I had the good fortune of partaking in was Cyndi Lauper's spine-tingling rendition of *I'm Gonna Be Strong*. I got goose bumps every time we performed that song. She is very underrated as a vocalist.

Performance Tips

- During the "A" and "C" sections of the chart, the snare drum and the floor tom are played together on beat 4 of each measure. Make sure they are played exactly at the same time without flamming.
- The development of a clean, consistent side stick sound is essential.
- Pay attention to the tuning of your drums when playing a rock ballad. More often than not, tuning your drums lower will fit a ballad better than higher pitched tuning.
- Rock ballads often require the drummer to raise the dynamic level when entering a chorus with a big fill. These fills should be simple, wide-open fills that contain a lot of space, not a lot of clutter.
- Maintain control over dynamics. You may be required to play very softly (verses) to very loudly (choruses) during the same tune. The tempo **must** stay consistent during these shifts in dynamic levels. One way to practice this is to play three bars, at 55 bpm very softly, play a big, open fill in bar 4 into three bars played very loudly, a fill in bar 4 back to three bars of very soft playing etc.
- Listen to the lyrics and play what you feel fits the mood of them.
- Rehearse the eighth-note ballad groove, including fills with a metronome paying special attention to very slow tempos.

Class Notes:

14

Rock Ballad

♩ = 75

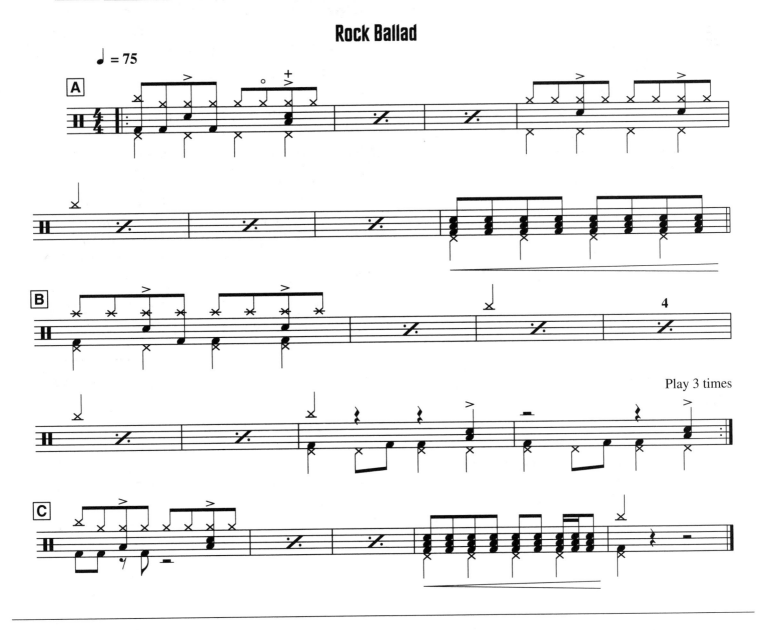

Play 3 times

Demo Roadmap
A, B, C

Chart Roadmap
A-B (3X), C

Class Notes: _____
_____
_____

Rock Ballad Variations

Selected Recorded Examples

Angel – Aerosmith
Don't Let the Sun Go Down on Me – Elton John
Every Time You Go Away – Paul Young
I Wanna Know What Love Is - Foreigner
I'm Gonna Be Strong – Cyndi Lauper
Imagine – John Lennon
In the Air Tonight – Phil Collins
Into the Night – Benny Mardones
People Get Ready – Rod Stewart
The First Cut is the Deepest – Rod Stewart
Wonderful Tonight – Eric Clapton

Class Notes: _____
_____
_____

SUB-STYLE NO. 4:
Funk Rock

Brief History

There is a reason we call him "The Godfather of Soul." James Brown spawned the funk movement in the early 60s with the release of *Live at the Apollo* (1963). "The hardest working man in show business" and his band *The JB's* had a sound that featured tight, clean rhythm guitars, syncopated horn parts, simple chord arrangements and an infectious rhythm that centered around the "one" of the measure. If you didn't move to this music, you were dead!

Sly and the Family Stone combined funk, rock, pop and a bit of the psychedelic sound of their native San Francisco Bay area to create a whole new sound that crossed over into pop radio. Their sound featured tight horn parts, keyboards (piano and Hammond B-3), simple chord arrangements and a strong backbeat. Some of the groups/artists that followed that have a "rock/pop edge" to their funk are Prince, Stevie Wonder, Extreme, The Red Hot Chili Peppers, The Average White Band, Earth, Wind and Fire, The Jacksons, Kool and the Gang, KC and the Sunshine Band, The Power Station and Tower of Power to name a few.

With simplification of some of its rhythms, applying a quarter-note bass-drum rhythm, funk became the basis for disco music of the 70s.

Performance Tips

- Note that in the A section of the play-along chart the snare is placed on the "and" of 2 and 4.
- When playing the open/closed hi-hat during the A and C sections of the chart, close it tightly. The sound has to be clean, crisp and tight, like the style.
- All the bass-drum notes have to be clearly enunciated. If the tempo of the chart prevents you from playing it cleanly, set your metronome at a slower tempo to execute it cleanly. Then gradually increase the bpm to the tempo of the chart.
- Play the ghost notes softly and the backbeat loudly.
- Rehearse all options with a metronome at various tempos.

Class Notes: _____

_____

Class Notes: _____

_____

Funk Rock

Demo Roadmap
A, B, C

Chart Roadmap
A-B (3X), C

Class Notes: _____
_____
_____

Funk Rock Variations

Selected Recorded Examples

1999 – Prince
Get the Funk Out – Extreme
Give It Away – Red Hot Chili Peppers
Jungle Boogie – Kool & The Gang
Pick up the Pieces – Average White Band
Sing a Simple Song – Sly and the Family Stone
Some Like It Hot – Power Station
Superstitious – Stevie Wonder
Thank You (Falettinme Be Mice Elf Agin) – Sly and the Family Stone
What Is Hip? – Tower of Power
What You Need - INXS

Class Notes: _____

Class Notes: _____

Class Notes: _____

Class Notes: _____

SUB-STYLE NO. 5:
Heavy Rock (Double Bass Drums)

Brief History

After the swing pulse straightened out into eighth notes with a backbeat (1950s) the tempos got slower and bands utilized "riffs" as the framework to their songs. The drums provided a "bed" upon which the riff and melody could rest. The music now had a "heavy feel" to it. AC/DC and Led Zeppelin were, and still remain, two of the most popular bands that brought this style to the masses.

The first drummer to implement the use of double bass drums was Louis Bellson in the 1940s. However, it wasn't until the 60s and 70s that "double kicks" were brought to the mainstream by drummers like Ginger Baker (Cream), Carmine Appice (Vanilla Fudge), Ansley Dunbar (Ansley Dunbar Retaliation) and Keith Moon (The Who). "Moony," as he was called, used the second kick drum for "show"—he didn't play it at all. Later on Simon Phillips, Lars Ulrich, Steve Smith and Virgil Donati, among others, took the double kicks to another level.

The main challenge facing double bass drummers today is the temptation to overuse them and keeping the tempo steady when we do use them appropriately.

Performance Tips

Heavy Rock

- The execution of a clean, consistent rim shot is essential in playing heavy rock. The term "heavy" means playing in medium to medium-slow tempos with the emphasis on the rim- shot back beat placed slightly behind the beat accompanied by a simple, sparse kick-drum pattern. The drumming in the greatest heavy-rock songs is simple and played with confidence and attitude. Every note should be clean and played in consistent tempo. "Seek the note."
- Tuning your drums lower and deeper fits this style.

Double Bass Drums

- Pay special attention to the click when making the transition between the single-bass drum and double-bass drums sections of the chart. The tendency is to move ahead of the click when making this transition. The following exercise will help: Play two bars of a single-bass drum beat into two bars of a double-bass drums beat. Use sixteenth notes and eighth-note triplets as your double-bass beat.
- When playing double-bass drums, start very slowly, paying close attention to the evenness of the right and left bass-drum sound. Stay relaxed. Record your rehearsal to check the balance of the sound between your left and right feet, and between your hands and feet. Start by playing steady eighth notes, then sixteenths, then eighth-note triplets. When you are comfortable with these steady note patterns, move on to the double-bass drums options I've provided.
- Have fun and remember, pick and choose your utilization of double bass drums in songs very carefully. Play for the song, not your chops!

Heavy Rock (Double Bass Drums)

Demo Roadmap
A1, A2, B1, B2 (First 4 bars of each)

Chart Roadmap
A1-A2-B1-B2 (2X)

Heavy Rock (Double Bass Drums) Variations

Sixteenth-Notes

Eighth-Note Triplets with Ride Bell

Optional Ride Patterns

Sixteenth-Note Triplets

Selected Recorded Examples

Heavy Rock:
Back in Black - AC/DC
Goin' Down – Jeff Beck Group
I La, La Love You – Pat Travers Band
Kashmir – Led Zeppelin
Love in an Elevator – Aerosmith
Runnin' with the Devil - Van Halen
The Stroke- Billy Squire
The Wonton Song – Led Zeppelin
Vertigo – U2

Double Bass Drums:
Master of Puppets – Metallica
One – Metallica
Parchment Farm – Cactus
Skin Deep – Duke Ellington/Louie Bellson
Space Boogie – Jeff Beck
Who'll Take the Fall – Pat Travers Band

SUB-STYLE NO. 3:
Traditional Shuffle

Brief History

As I mentioned before, the swing pulse is the common denominator of all American music. We can trace it back to Ragtime (early 1900s), New Orleans Jazz (1900s–1930s), Big Band Swing (1930s), Bebop (1940s) and Rhythm & Blues (Late 40s into the early 50s).

In the late 40s the existing acoustic American-roots styles—Blues, Country and Gospel—started incorporating the drum kit as a way to commercialize the music and expose it to a larger audience. The drummers on the early Country, Gospel and Blues recordings were all experienced Jazz drummers, at the time they were hired for the sessions. Since the pulse of American-roots music was a swing feel, the Jazz drummers adapted easily. The young drummers of the day who were listening to and inspired by these recordings grew up wanting to be Country drummers, Blues drummers, Gospel drummers and Rock drummers, depending on the musical style they were interested in.

The ability to play a strong, consistent shuffle that contains a bouncy swing pulse is the heart of any good Rock drummer or any type of drummer for that matter.

Performance Tips

- Maintain a quarter-note left foot (heel) hi-hat pattern throughout. When riding on the closed hi-hat, your left heel maintains the quarter pulse.
- Develop a strong "2 & 4" backbeat (rim shot).
- Play at many different tempos with a metronome, with special attention given to slower tempos.
- 2 & 4 backbeat should be loud and ghost notes soft.
- Experiment with playing on different areas of the snare drum to create a variety of sounds, for example, ghost notes near the edge of the head and the accented backbeat at the center of the head.
- Try using different textures on the snare. For example, use blastics: shuffle on the snare with the right hand and play the backbeat with the left.
- When playing the "double-handed shuffle" on the hi-hat and snare, loosen the hi-hat cymbals up a bit to create a "swishy" sound. Control this sound dynamically to differentiate between the different sections of the song.
- Practice the traditional shuffle with a metronome at various tempos, paying special attention to the slower tempos and challenging yourself with the faster ones.
- Drums tuned higher in pitch fits this sub-style the best.

Class Notes: _____

_____

_____

Traditional Shuffle

Demo Roadmap

Intro, A, C

Chart Roadmap

Intro, A-B (2X), C

Traditional Shuffle Variations

Selected Recorded Examples

Before You Accuse Me – Eric Clapton
Cold Shot – Stevie Ray Vaughn
Hideaway – Freddie King, Johnny Winter
Highway 61 Revisited – Johnny Winter
I Got My Eye on You – Buddy Guy
Let Me Love You – Stevie Ray Vaughn
Let the Good Times Roll – B.B. King
She Likes to Boogie Real Low – Johnny Winter
Talk to Me Baby – Elmore James
Watch Yourself – B.B. King

SUB-STYLE NO. 7:
Hard Rock Shuffle

Brief History

In the 60s when rock developed a harder edge to it and drummers were moving to the forefront both sonically and visually, the Hard Rock Shuffle was born. It is characterized by a strong backbeat and a syncopated bass-drum pattern that often aligned itself with the bass guitar part of the song.

A few of the best examples of rock shuffles are tunes that I did with The Pat Travers Band, *Rockin'* and *Boom Boom (Out Go the Lights)*, and with Michael Bolton *Without Your Love*.

Performance Tips
- Keep a solid, consistent backbeat at all times.
- When ghost notes are used, play them softly and the backbeat loudly, to create a nice contrast in dynamics.
- All bass-drum notes should be clean and even.

Class Notes: _____

Class Notes: _____

Class Notes: _____

Hard Rock Shuffle

Demo Roadmap

Intro, A, B, C

Chart Roadmap

Intro, A-B (2X), C

Hard Rock Shuffle Variations

Add Ghost Notes

Selected Recorded Examples

Boom Boom (Out Go the Lights) – Pat Travers Band
Can't Get Enough – Bad Company
I Ain't Superstitious – Jeff Beck/Rod Stewart
Smokin' in the Boys Room – Brownsville Station
Tie Your Mother Down – Queen
Tush – ZZ Top
Without Your Love – Michael Bolton (Blackjack)

SUB-STYLE NO. 8:
$\frac{12}{8}$ Slow Blues

Brief History

The Blues originated sometime after the Civil War as a result of rhythms and "call and answer" chants brought over by slaves from Africa. During the 1920s and 30s, songs by such blues pioneers as Robert Johnson and Lightnin' Hopkins were spread by radio across the south. In the 30s and 40s the blues was urbanized and electrified by such artists as Muddy Waters, John Lee Hooker and Elmore James in places such as Chicago, Memphis, Detroit and Houston.

By the early 60s these urban bluesmen were ""discovered" by white musicians in America and England. As a result, artists such as John Mayall's Bluesbreakers, The Paul Butterfield Blues Band, The Yardbirds, The Stones, Led Zeppelin, The Jimi Hendrix Experience, Cream and Fleetwood Mac exposed the blues to young, white audiences in the United States and Europe. Today, people like Buddy Guy and B.B. King carry on the blues tradition.

In the 60s when bands such as Led Zeppelin and The Jimi Hendrix Experience played a "rockified" brand of the blues aided by Marshall stacks, Fender Stratocasters and 26" kick drums, they took the blues off the front porch of a roadside shack in Tupelo and moved it to the pyro-enhanced arena stage.

Performance Tips

- Become comfortable with playing the $\frac{12}{8}$ feel at very slow tempos. Use a metronome and its triplet subdivision if available.
- Don't rush this feel! Let the backbeat come to you!
- Try this "Mr. Good Timekeeper:" Set the metronome to quarter notes at 35 bpm. Right Hand Triplet ride; left hand 2-4 snare/bass drum 1-3. Then try it with quarter right hand ride, crash every four measures. Wow.
- Substitute the side stick for the full snare sound in the A-section of the chart. Give attention to a clean transition from side stick in the A-section, crash then full snare in the B-section.
- At bar 11—the B-section—build gradually over the course of one measure.
- Use optional ending.
- While playing the "options" beats, play ghost notes lightly and back beat heavily where indicated. Open and close the hi-hat crisply and cleanly where indicated.

Class Notes: _____

_____

_____

Demo Roadmap

First 4 bars of A
Last 8 bars of B

Chart Roadmap

Intro, A, B

$\frac{12}{8}$ Slow Blues Variations

Selected Recorded Examples

Dazed and Confused – Led Zeppelin
Night Prowler – AC/DC
Red House – The Jimi Hendrix Experience
Since I've Been Loving' You – Led Zeppelin
When My Heart Starts Beatin' – B.B. King/Eric Clapton
You Shook Me – Jeff Beck/Rod Stewart

Class Notes: _____

_____

_____

SUB-STYLE NO. 3:
2-Beat

Brief History

The 2-beat groove has its roots in country, gospel and early swing music. Country drummers used the 2-beat swing feel in the late 30s and 40s. The drummers of the day used brushes on the snare to produce the groove with little or no use of cymbals. Rock and R&B artists first incorporated the 2-beat swing into their music in the early 50s. This evolved into the eighth-note 2-beat feel in the middle to late 50s.

One reason I value The Monkees' gig so much is that it gives me the opportunity to play a diverse spectrum of musical styles, simply because they have had many different songwriters write for them. One of the better-known Monkees' songs that contain a 2-beat feel is *Papa Jeans Blues,* which is a country song, not a blues. *Rollin' and Tumblin,* a blues classic that I performed with Johnny Winter, and *Can't Judge a Book* by Bo Diddley remain two of my all-time favorite examples of a 2-beat.

Performance Tips

- The kick-drum part is often dictated by the bass-guitar part and vice versa. So open your ears and listen! Make sure what you play on the kick drum is aligned with the bass-guitar part; **no flamming.**
- Keep the tempo steady. The tendency is to rush the 2-beat, especially after a fill.
- A good exercise for this is to play four measures of straight time (two and four backbeat) into four measures of 2-beat (backbeat on all the "ands"). This exercise must be done with a metronome at various tempos.
- The development of a rim shot is essential to attain a broad range of dynamic texture to this and all rock sub-styles.
- Maintain a steady, uninterrupted left foot hi-hat part, either on the downbeat or the upbeat. Whichever you choose, be sure it's consistent, especially during beat-fill-beat transitions.

Class Notes: _____

Class Notes: _____

2-Beat

Demo Roadmap
A, B, C

Chart Roadmap
A-B (4X), C

2-Beat Variations

Selected Recorded Examples

Bron-Y-Aur Stomp – Led Zeppelin
Can't Judge a Book – Bo Diddley
I'm Walkin' – Fats Domino
Papa Gene's Blues – The Monkees
Rollin and Tumblin' – Johnny Winter
Viva Las Vegas – Elvis Presley
What'd I Say? – Ray Charles
When the Saints Go Marchin' In – Fats Domino

SUB-STYLE NO. 10:
Train Beat (Country Shuffle)

Brief History

The Train Beat, sometimes called a Country Shuffle, is a variation of the 2-beat groove that has origins in country, bluegrass and gospel music. It has since grown in popularity to include rock and pop, Cajun and rockabilly.

It is played with sixteenths on the snare with the accent on the upbeat (the "and" of 1, 2, 3, 4). The bass-drum pattern is usually played on the downbeat to accompany the 2-beat bass line.

It is also possible to play the accent on the "2" and "4" while playing the sixteenths on the snare, as in the Bob Seeger song *Hollywood Nights*.

There are variations for the snare accents and kick patterns as demonstrated in the "variations" section.

Performance Tips

- Use "Blasticks", "Hot Rods" or brushes as alternatives to sticks.
- Play unaccented notes softly and accented notes loudly.
- Utilize the rim shot for an even louder dynamic, for example during solos and choruses.
- Keep it simple, and do not overplay. As always, be sensitive to the vocal and/or the instrumentalist that is soloing. Stay out of the way.
- The kick-drum pattern usually locks in with the bass guitar. Listen and react!
- Experiment with playing the snare part on different areas of the head; near the rim, in the center of the head etc.
- Maintain the steady upbeat, left-foot, hi-hat pattern.
- Pay attention to the difference in the accented patterns from the A-section to the B- section and the slightly different kick-drum pattern in the B-section.
- Rehearse this groove with a metronome at various tempos.
- Often, it is appropriate to play the Train Beat (Country Shuffle) "on top of the beat." This gives the beat a "forward motion," which is sometimes what tunes that use the train beat require. Playing on "top of the beat" does NOT mean rushing the tempo.

Class Notes: _____

Class Notes: _____

37

Train Beat (Country Shuffle)

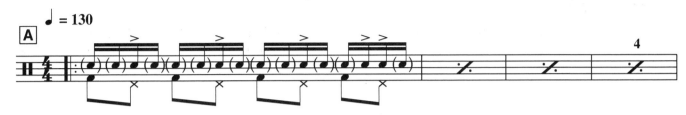

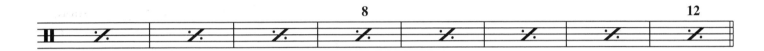

Demo Roadmap
A, B, C

Chart Roadmap
A-B (4X), C

Class Notes: _____

_____

_____

Train Beat (Country Shuffle) Variations

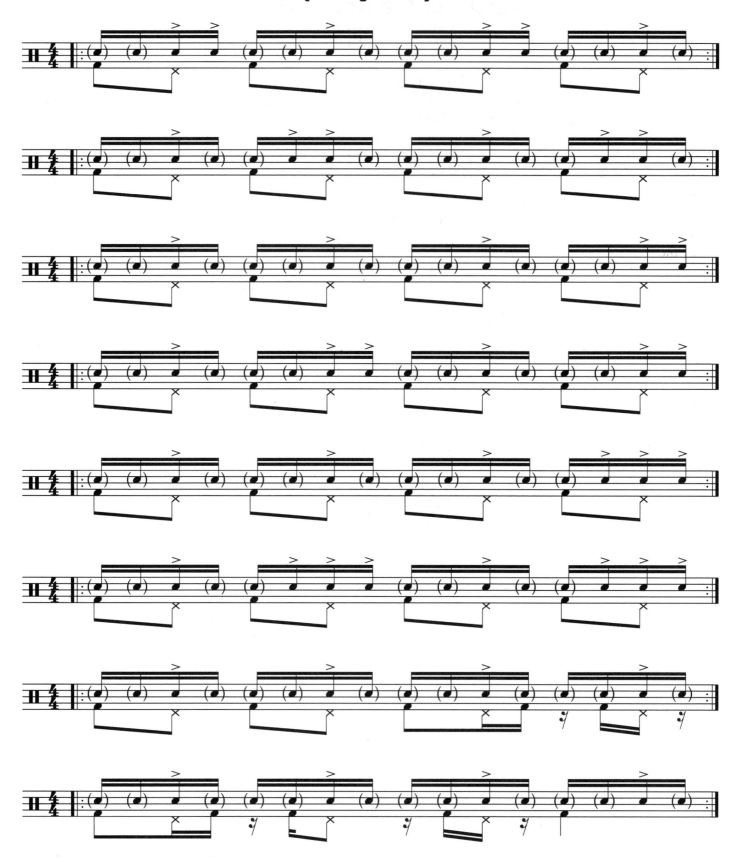

Selected Recorded Examples

Folsom Prison Blues – Johnny Cash
Gallows Pole – Led Zeppelin
Hollywood Nights – Bob Seeger
On the Road Again – Willie Nelson
Train Time – Cream
Trouble on the Line – Sawyer Brown

SUB-STYLE NO. 11:
"Bo Diddley" Beat

Brief History

I've had the honor and pleasure of touring with Bo Diddley since 2002. I have gained a tremendous amount of knowledge from this Rock 'n' Roll Hall of Fame Legend both on and off the stage. The highlight of our gigs together is when he comes back to my drums during the song *Hey Bo Diddley*. He stands next to me to my right, over my floor tom, grabs a pair of sticks and we proceed to "trade fours" over a rockin' vamp of the "Bo Diddley" beat, for at least five minutes. It's magic.

There are a few schools of thought on the origination of the "Bo Diddley" beat. According to Bo himself, the "Bo Diddley" Beat came to him as a result of being inspired by the rhythms of the Caribbean and Africa and the rhythmic chants that often accompanied African music. The "Bo Diddley" Beat is identified by the same accents as a 3:2 clave, which is contained in Afro-Cuban music. It is also a rhythm influenced by "hambone," a style used by African-American street musicians to play out the rhythm by slapping and patting their arms, legs, chest and cheeks while chanting over it. The style is defined by a repetitive catchy, rhythm played under chant or rap vocal phrasing in songs that sometimes had no chord changes! (*Hey Bo Diddley* and *Who Do You Love?*).

Bo Diddley was born in the Mississippi Delta and raised between there and the south side of Chicago. When we play a $\frac{12}{8}$ (*I'm A Man*) or a bright 2-beat (*Who Do You Love?*) or an even brighter train beat (*You can't Judge a Book by Its Cover*) to a great bouncy traditional shuffle (*Before You Accuse Me*) into a hard-rockin' medium eighth-note feel (*Road Runner*), it's always an education. Incidentally, he wrote all of these classic songs.

I am learning from the master who is considered one of the founding fathers of Rock. He has had a direct influence on a virtual Who's Who of musicians and songwriters, as evidenced by the amount of times his songs have been covered by other artists, not to mention the number of times his famous rhythm has been used as the basis for the songs of other songwriters.

I am fortunate to have the opportunity to share stages worldwide with this man. For that I am grateful.

Performance Tips

- SWING those sixteenths! Work on getting in that awesome pocket between straight eighths and swung triplets.
- Playing your left foot hi-hat as an upbeat opposite the quarter-note downbeat of the kick drum greatly enhances the feel of the "Diddley" beat. (Sections A and C)
- Play the accented sixteenth-note rhythm on your rack tom, NOT your floor tom, as requested by Mr. Diddley himself.
- The accented sixteenths are played as single strokes.
- Keep it simple and strong. Ignore any temptation to "frill it up" by playing some sort of a "ruff" prior to the "one" of the measure.
- When there are vocals present, place crashes around them, not over them.
- In section B, give attention to the kick-drum pattern, specifically the "e- and" of 3. Be sure they are even in sound. If they are not, rehearse with the metronome at a slower tempo and build up the chart tempo (102bpm).
- Close the hi-hat tightly on the "one" following the opening of it on the "and" of 4.
- Experiment with ghost notes when playing the "Bo Diddley" beat in "beat" form as in option beat no. 2.
- Play ghost notes softly and the backbeat louder with the rim shot as an option.
- When playing the "Bo Diddley" rhythm in "beat" form (kick, snare and hi-hat), lay back on it, relax and don't rush it.
- Gain the discipline of playing a rhythm like this for long periods of time, with no frills and continually making it feel good.
- An interesting implementation of the "Bo Diddley" Beat by double-bass drummers could be found in option beat no. 7 on page 42. A metal-tube shaker works best for the right-hand part. Also, play the double-bass drum part lower in volume than the left-hand accents on the snare and toms.

Note: There are two common ways to notate the "Bo Diddley" Beat: 1) with accents placed over two measures of eighth notes, and 2) with accents placed over one measure of sixteenth notes. I chose to notate this example with sixteenth notes. I wanted the kick drum part to be interpreted as four quarter notes under one cycle of the rhythm (i.e. in the A and C sections).

"Bo Diddley" Beat

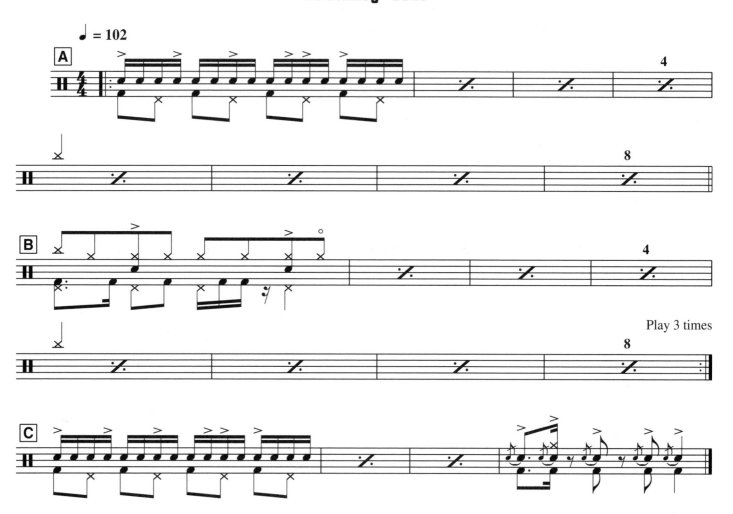

Demo Roadmap
A, B, C

Chart Roadmap
A-B (3X), C

"Bo Diddley" Beat Variations

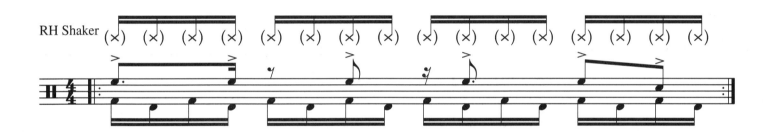

Selected Recorded Examples

Desire – U2
Faith – George Michael
Hey Bo Diddley – Bo Diddley
Hey Little Girl - Dee Clark
I Want Candy – The Strangelove's
Magic Bus – The Who
Not Fade Away – The Rolling Stones, Buddy Holly
Poor Tom – Led Zeppelin
She's the One – Bruce Springsteen
Willie and the Hand Jive – Johnny Otis, Eric Clapton

SUB-STYLE NO. 12:
New Orleans Second Line

Brief History

At the mouth of the Mississippi, New Orleans has stood at a crossroads where French, Spanish, English, African, Caribbean and Latin-American cultures have met and mixed for over two centuries. Its culture has helped shape the sound of R&B, Rock, Delta Blues, Jazz and Ragtime.

In the 40s artists like Professor Longhair combined the loose artistry of jazz with the "second-line" syncopations and raucous brass work of Mardi Gras parade bands. There are a few differing opinions regarding the origin of the term "second-line" drumming. One is that there was a line of musicians (i.e., the second line) that marched behind the first line of mourners in a funeral parade. The other explanation is that there was a secondary rhythm section (second line) that answered the calls of the first-line rhythm section in a New Orleans Mardi Gras parade. One thing is certain: "second-line" drumming involves marching snare-drum rhythms. A descendant of second-line drumming involves the combination of funk drumming, second-line traditional New Orleans marches and the 3:2 clave feel of the "Bo Diddley" beat. This fusion of styles was made popular by, but not limited to such artists as The Meters, The Neville Brothers, Little Feat and Dr. John.

Performance Tips

- The entire chart is played on the snare drum with the snares "off."
- The A-section of the chart is simply the "Bo Diddley" beat with the accents played on the kick drum as well as the snare.
- The thirty-second-note "ruff" that's played prior to the "1" in sections A and C of the chart as well as in some "variation" beats must be played cleanly and in time in order to achieve its desired effect. This "ruff" is played on the "and of 4" and can be executed using an open or closed roll.
- Utilize the rim shot for the accents when a louder dynamic is indicated.
- Maintain the quarter-note, left-foot hi-hat part throughout. For a slightly different feel, play the left-foot hi-hat part on the upbeat (ands) of each quarter note.

Class Notes: _____

_____

_____

New Orleans Second Line
CD Track #23 Demo / Track #24 Play-along

New Orleans Second Line

Demo Roadmap
A, B, C

Chart Roadmap
A-B (3X), C

Class Notes: _____

_____

_____

New Orleans Second Line Variations

Selected Recorded Examples

Cissy Strut – The Meters
Hey Pocky Way – The Neville Brothers
Iko, Iko – Dr. John
Look-Ka Py Py – The Meters
Willie and the Hand Jive – Johnny Otis, Eric Clapton

Class Notes: _____

_____

_____

Class Notes: _____

_____

_____

SUB-STYLE NO. 13:
Up-tempo Rock-Swing with Stop Time (Rockabilly)

Brief History

It has been stated that we can trace the swing pulse all the way back to the Civil War, the plantation fields of the deep South and the plains of Africa. It has since been adapted to the rock style with a little taste of country, gospel, rockabilly and blues, depending on the particular artist.

For me, few songs have been more fun to play than The Monkees version of the high-spirited, rock-swing with stop time tune *Goin' Down*. It really ROCKS!

The key to a high-tempo, rock-swing tune is keeping the meter consistent and the groove simple. Keep it cookin'!

Performance Tips

- Be sure the transition is clean and tight between sections A (full snare) and section B (side stick).
- The opening and closing of the hi-hat in section B should be clean and crisp. It may be difficult at first because the tempo is so "up" (240 bpms). If this is the case, set the metronome at a slower tempo, say at 180 and play the chart again. Then again at 190, then 200 etc.
- Pay special attention to the consistency of the tempo during the stop-time section of the chart.
- Keep time throughout the stop time and four measures of rest (with cymbal choke) at the very end of the chart.

Class Notes: _____

Class Notes: _____

Up-tempo Rock-Swing with Stop Time

Demo Roadmap
A, B, C

Chart Roadmap
A-B (3X), C

Up-tempo Rock-Swing with Stop-Time Variations

Optional Ride Pattern on Hi-hat

Selected Recorded Examples

Crazy Little Thing Called Love – Queen
Goin' Down – The Monkees
Jump, Jive and Wail – The Brian Setzer Orchestra
Route 66 – The Brian Setzer Orchestra
That's Alright Mama – Elvis Presley
The Dirty Boogie – The Brian Setzer Orchestra

SUB-STYLE NO. 1½:
Reggae (Shuffle Feel)

Brief History

Before the 1940s, the music popular with Jamaica's poor majority was called "Mento." Mento was sung and played on guitars and percussion, and was derived from the Jamaican's African heritage, local work songs, spirituals, calypso, rhumba and merengue rhythms of neighboring islands. By the late 40s and early 50s, American R&B began to make an impression on Jamaicans via radio from Memphis, New Orleans and Miami.

By the early 1960s, Jamaican artists developed an original sound by combining Mento- styled songs with the R&B groove and arrangements for horns, keyboards, electric guitars, drums and bass.

Reggae's distinctive sound was achieved by reversing the traditional instrumental roles: the guitar functioned mainly as a rhythm instrument, scratching chords on the upbeat. The bass played a melodic counterpart to the vocal melody line, and the drums provided a "bed" of a simple and repetitive groove. The rhythms existed in a straight eighth or shuffle feel.

A good example of a reggae rock song with a shuffle feel is a Bob Marley song I recorded and performed live with The Pat Travers Band called *Is This Love*?. It is played using a "four drop-shuffle feel" (see **Performance Tips** below for a definition of this term).

The term "Reggae" was the name given in 1968 to the latest in a succession of Jamaican dance rhythms, but the term has come to refer to the various styles derived from the Afro-Caribbean music and American R&B that have flourished in Jamaica since the early 1960s.

Performance Tips

- This Reggae play-along is performed using a shuffle feel. In both sections A and B there are two-measure phrases that repeat.
- The feel in section A is known as a "one-drop" with one note played on the kick drum per measure. The feel in section B is known as a "four-drop" or "steppers." This is when there are steady quarter notes played on the kick drum (four per measure) in $\frac{4}{4}$ time.
- Execute a clean transition between the side-stick groove in section A and the full-snare groove of section B.
- Become accustomed to counting repetitive measures of any chart to yourself instead of having your eyes "glued" to the chart measure by measure. This frees you up to concentrate on the feel and consistency of what you are playing, instead of the notes on a page.
- Play the right hand hi-hat part with the tip of the stick, instead of the shoulder of the stick to create a lighter, more "bouncy" feel, instead of a heavy, "plodding" feel.
- Make sure the open/closed hi-hat part in section B is executed cleanly and crisply.
- Playing fills in a Reggae feel is interesting because oftentimes the "one" is absent from the measure following the fill. This creates a space, gap or "hole" around beat 1 of that measure. Don't feel you have to fill it; let it remain a space. This is part of Reggae's unique feel.

Reggae (Shuffle Feel)

Demo Roadmap
A, B

Chart Roadmap
A-B (2X)

Class Notes: _____

_____

_____

Reggae (Shuffle Feel) Variations

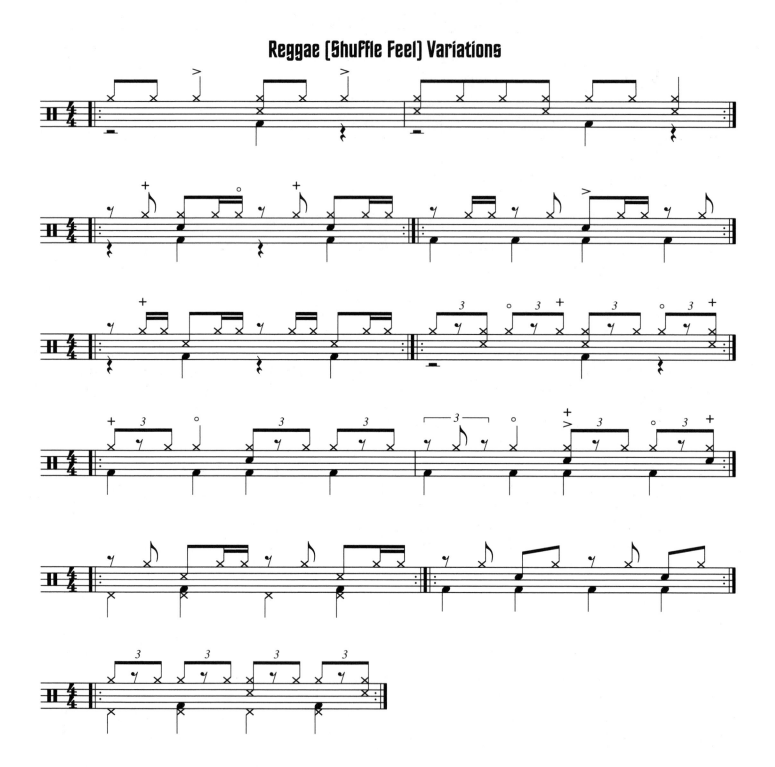

Selected Recorded Examples

Every Little Thing She Does Is Magic – The Police
Give It to Me – The J. Geils Band
I Shot the Sheriff – Eric Clapton
Is This Love? – Bob Marley, The Pat Travers Band
Master Blaster – Stevie Wonder
Mother and Child Reunion – Paul Simon
The Tide Is High – Blondie
Walking on the Moon – The Police

SUB-STYLE NO. 15:
Rockin' Odd Meters

Brief History

The history of drumming in odd time correlates directly with the history of jazz and swing. It wasn't until the 70s that musicians "fused" elements of jazz, rock, funk and classical into "Fusion" music or its more commercial counterpart "Progressive" music. They also incorporated music from other cultures such as the Caribbean, South America and India. This music is very chops-oriented with odd-time signatures being very common. Miles Davis was a pioneer of jazz-rock fusion by using electric instruments to fuse together funk and rock with lengthy jazz improvisations.

As the amount of notes musicians played grew substantially, so did the drum kits. It was not uncommon for a fusion drum kit to contain two bass drums, six to eight rack toms, ten or more cymbals, and seemingly every percussion "toy" in existence. "China type" cymbals grew in popularity during this period.

There is (was) a tendency by some artists to be highly technical in the making of their music entirely for technique sake, to "outplay" the next guy or to be "faster" on their instrument than anyone else. If played with this misguided motivation, the music becomes very sterile, like a tile room with bright, florescent lights, very UN-rock. It should be all about the SONGS played with feeling, emotion and heart. While technique is important — it aids in the manifestation of your musical ideas — it shouldn't be your prime motivation in making music.

Performance Tips

- The odd-time chart has quarter notes played with the right hand on the bell of the ride cymbal throughout the entire chart. This will facilitate counting the odd time signature as you play it. If playing odd time is new to you, start by just playing the quarter-note bell ride pattern accompanied by the "1" of each measure played on the kick drum. COUNT!
- While familiarizing yourself with the concept of playing odd time, it is sometimes helpful to "sandwich" the odd-time measure between measures of $\frac{4}{4}$ time. One measure $\frac{4}{4}$, one measure odd etc.
- Experiment with different ways of counting odd-time measures. For example, in a measure of $\frac{7}{4}$, the counting options are, 1-2-3-4-5-6-7 or 1-2-3-4, 1-2-3 or 1-2,1-2,1-2-3.
- During the B-section of the odd-time chart, I recommend counting it 1-2-3, 1-2-3-4. Counting in this manner correlates with the riff of the tune.
- While playing the B-section $\frac{7}{4}$ and the C-section $\frac{5}{4}$, crash on the "1" to "announce" the start of each measure as indicated on the chart.

Class Notes:

52

Rockin' Odd Meters

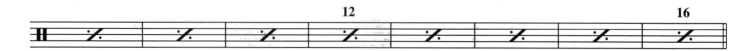

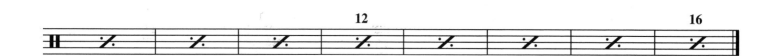

Demo Roadmap
A, B, C

Chart Roadmap
A-B (3X), C

Class Notes: _____

_____

_____

Rockin' Odd Meter Variations

Selected Recorded Examples
All You Need Is Love – The Beatles
Lucky Man – Emerson, Lake & Palmer
Manic Depression – The Jimi Hendrix Experience
The Ocean – Led Zeppelin
Tom Sawyer – Rush
Turn It on Again – Genesis
White Room – Cream

Selected Bibliography (Books/DVDs)

Appice, Carmine. *Realistic Rock* (Warner Bros.).

Chester, Gary. *The New Breed* (Modern Drummer Publications).

Lauren, Michael and Rondinelli, Bobby. *The Encyclopedia of Double Bass Drumming* (Hal Leonard Publications)

Rothman, Joel. *Basic Drumming* (JR Publications).

————. *Rock Breaks around the Drums* (JR Publications).

Smith, Steve. *Drumset Technique/History of the U.S. Beat* (Hudson Music DVD).

Stone, George Lawrence. *Stick Control.* (George B. Stone & Son)

Zoro. *10 Commandments of R&B Drumming* (Warner Bros Book & DVD).

Selected Discography

AC/DC – *Back in Black* (Atlantic)

B.B King – *King of the Blues* (MCA)

Bo Diddley – *20ᵗʰ Anniversary* (RCA)

Booker T. & the MGs – *The Best of* (Atlantic)

Chuck Berry – *Greatest Hits* (Chess)

Cream – *The Very Best of Cream* (Polydor)

Eric Clapton – *From the Cradle* (Warner Bros)

James Brown – *20 All-time Greatest Hits* (Polydor)

Jeff Beck – *Beckology* (Epic/Legacy)

Jerry Lee Lewis – *The Best of* (Smash)

Jimi Hendrix – *The Essential Jimi Hendrix* (Reprise)

Johnny Winter – *Johnny Winter and Live* (Columbia)

Led Zeppelin Box Set – (Atlantic)

Little Richard – *The Very Best of Little Richard* (UA)

Muddy Waters – *They Call Me Muddy Waters* (Chess)

Rolling Stones – *40 Licks* (ABKCO/Virgin)

Sly and the Family Stone – *Greatest Hits* (Epic)

The Beatles – *Abbey Road* (Apple)

The Police – *Synchronicity* (A&M)

The Who – *Who's Next?* (MCA)

GLOSSARY OF MUSICAL TERMS

Accent. Emphasis placed on a particular note as to give it more volume than the others around it,

Backbeat. A consistent rhythm that accents beats 2 and 4 in a measure of $\frac{4}{4}$ time. In other time signatures the backbeat will land elsewhere. For example, in a $\frac{12}{8}$ slow blues feel, the backbeat lands on the fourth and tenth eighth note of the measure. A "Fatback" backbeat is a thick, slightly behind-the-beat backbeat that oozes feel. R&B, funk, soul, and certain kinds of rock can contain this awesome brand of backbeat.

BPMs. An acronym that stands for the "Beats per Minute" setting on the metronome, drum machine or click track. It's the number of quarter notes that transpire in one minute.

Common or $\frac{4}{4}$ time. Four beats to the measure with the quarter note receiving the value of one beat.

Downbeat. Among the eight eighth notes in a bar of $\frac{4}{4}$ time, beats 1, 2, 3 and 4 would be considered the downbeat. The "and" of 1, "and" of 2, "and" of 3, and "and" of 4 are the upbeats. Similar to the arm motion of orchestral conductor.

Dynamics. Playing in varying degrees of volume on the drum kit in both long and short crescendos (increased volume) and decrescendos (decreased volume). We should have complete control over our playing in a variety of dynamic levels. Not only should we have control over the overall sound of the drumset, we should have control over the dynamic level of each individual limb as they relate to each other. For example, a loud dynamic on the kick and snare, a low dynamic on the hi-hat and ride cymbals.

Ghost Notes. Notes surrounded by parentheses () meant to be played very softly, in contrast to accented notes, notated with an accent >, which are meant to be played very loudly. Drummers should constantly strive to maintain and implement the widest spectrum of dynamic range in our playing style as possible.

Groove. A difficult to describe term, in the way that "feel" is difficult to describe. A drummer is groovin' when he's consistent, plays only what is appropriate for the song in a way that feels appropriate to him, his band and the audience. He becomes the heartbeat of the music. The body wants to move to the music. His drumming serves the song; the song does not serve his drumming.

Intro. The introduction of a song. It's possible to play the intro of a song more than once in the same song.

Kick Drum. Another word for the bass drum.

Marshall Stacks. A brand of guitar amplifier that gave the user the option of "stacking" the speaker cabinets one on top of the other as high as six feet. Jimi Hendrix, for example, used three Marshall stacks with two cabinets each being powered by up to 200 watts each!

Measure. The equal parts of which music is divided. Where the music is divided in relation to the notes depends on the time signature. Thin bar lines indicate the beginning and end of measures. A double bar line, one thin and one thick, indicates the end of an entire piece of music.

Odd-Time. Any time signature other than $\frac{4}{4}$ (common) time. The top number of the time signature indicates how many beats are in the measure. The bottom number indicates what note value receives one beat. For example, in $\frac{7}{4}$ time there are seven beats in the measure, and the quarter note receives one beat.

Outro. The counterpart to the "intro" of the song. The outro is the ending or last section of the song.

Pyro. An abbreviated version of the word pyrotechnics, which is the creation of fireworks and/or explosions for the purpose of entertainment. These are currently computer generated to correlate with the music being played.

Rehearsal or Section Letters. A capitalized A, B or C etc. utilized to indicate the beginning of a section of music. These sections are separated by two adjacent bar lines.

Repeat Signs. 1. Two dots placed before a double bar line, one thin, and one thick, means to go back to the opposite-facing sign and repeat. 2. A diagonal line with one dot on either side of it means to repeat the previous measure of music. 3. Two parallel diagonal lines with two dots on either side of them means to repeat the precious two measures of music.

Riff. Several notes played repetitively, in the same sequence to form the rhythmic foundation of a rock song. Two or more instruments usually riff together.

Rim Shot. Playing the rim and head of the drum at the same time This produces a louder, punchier more percussive sound especially when using flams to play the rim shot. Rim shots usually occur on the snare but could be played effectively on any drum of your kit.

Rock 'n' Roll. A blues euphemism for sexual intercourse.

Side Stick. The act of hitting the rim of the snare with the shoulder of the stick to produce a strong "click" sound. This is commonly used in ballads as an option to the full snare sound.

Time Signature. Noted at the beginning of a piece of music,, the time signature is written as a fraction. The top number indicates the number of beats in a measure and the lower number indicates what note value receives one beat as its value.

Trade Fours. When two or more musicians take turns at soloing for one or more measures of $\frac{4}{4}$.

Triplet. A common subdivision that uses groups of three notes per quarter-note pulse. These are called eighth-note triplets. Triplets can also be subdivided as quarter-note triplets and sixteenth-note triplets. Triplets are at the core of American Blues, R&B and Swing dating back to Dixieland and beyond. The correct way to count triplets is 1-trip-let, 2-trip-let, etc.

Upbeat. Among the eight eighth notes in a bar of $\frac{4}{4}$ time, the "and" of 1, "and" of 2, "and" of 3, and "and" of 4 would be considered the upbeat. Beats 1, 2, 3 and 4 would be considered the downbeat, similar to the arm motion of an orchestral conductor.